AL HELD 1959-1961

AL HELD 1959-1961

ESSAY BY IRVING SANDLER

ROBERT MILLER • APRIL 1980

724 FIFTH AVENUE, NEW YORK

AL HELD: 1959-1961

During the late 1950s, a crisis had developed within abstract expressionism or, more specifically, the painterly or gestural tendency within it. This manner had attracted so many mediocre followers and had become so glutted that it began to strike a small number of venturesome and ambitious young abstract artists, notably Al Held, Morris Louis, Kenneth Noland, and Frank Stella, as an overworked, academic, and stale dead end. They started to explore pictorial alternatives, aiming to embody individual visions in fresh, non-gestural, abstract styles.

In the case of Held, his was as much urgent style-growth as style-change. In 1959, he reviewed with a critical eye the abstractions he had painted in the previous four or five years—allover fields of pigment-laden, mainly earth-colored gestures. Held became aware that his artistic bent was toward clarity—a kind of classicizing urge. In his *pigment paintings,* he had tried without preconception to structure brush swaths into cogent designs, reconciling the competing demands of freedom and order. But in 1959, it was the designs that most engrossed him, and they were buried beneath the thick textures. However, incrusting his canvases with paint matter had enabled him to advance his surfaces into actual space, like tidal waves of impasto, and the idea of frontal projection continued to interest him[1]. Nevertheless, Held's primary need was to bring his infrastructures up to the surface and to articulate them—and since then, *articulate* has been a key word in his esthetic vocabulary. The ambiguous and unfinished trowelled and smeared slabs of paint would have to be cut through and cleaned up.

Wishing to proceed as freely and speedily as he could, Held

covered the walls of his studio with photographers' backdrop paper and changed his medium into quick drying liquitex. At that moment, there occurred an enormous release of energy and in the following six months, Held radically transformed his style. Instead of the heavy and loose facture and the dark palette of the *pigment paintings,* he brushed free-hand quasi-geometric and curvilinear configurations in flat, vivid color. In the first of these new pictures, as in the *pigment paintings,* the composition is *rhythmic* in that its components echo each other in shape and color. But Held would soon individuate them, that is, make each different from every other, a quality that he had just begun to achieve in the pictures on display. Held had *found* his form and his color.

Influencing Held's style-change was the painting of Matisse and Leger. Held often started by improvising with free shapes derived from Matisse's late cutouts, notably the *Jazz* series (reproduced in a book he owned). But after prolonged painting, and he insisted on repeated testing of the possibilities of his pictorial components, he ended up with mostly rectangles, triangles, and circles, turning a sensual biomorphism into a conceptual architecture and revealing a disposition for geometric structure that would predominate in time[2]. Today, Matisse's work is generally appreciated for its hedonistic and decorative qualities. But in the late 1950s, Held was inspired more by the toughness of the color and the taut surfaces of such pictures as *The Moroccans* at the Museum of Modern Art. Held also admired Leger's painting for its toughness, which surpassed Matisse's. In fact, he then spoke approvingly of Leger's *vulgarity.* He also began to see New York City as Leger did and introduced into his work a palette of *anti-melodic intensity* and *bad taste.*[3] By looking at Matisse with an eye to Leger, Held made his color stronger than that of both—a kind of visual noise; his

surfaces, more resistant, denser, and less airy; and his forms, more packed and muscular.

In the earlier of Held's *geometric* abstractions, the direct process of painting is clearly evident. That is, the forms are composed of visible brushstrokes. But the painterly gestures were soon suppressed, absorbed into the concrete forms of unmodulated colors that they shape. The color-forms and not the gestures came to bear the burden of content. Held soon discovered that through the action of color and the impacting of form, he could make his color-forms at once more immediate in their optical impact and volumetric so that they would appear to thrust out in a kind of inverse illusionism – more powerfully than had the *pigment paintings*.

Held recognized that piled-on paint got in the way of color, and he reduced the impasto, but he also perceived that the tangibility of his packed color-forms could contribute to their outward projection. Moreover, he was impelled by temperament toward physicality (as were his close friends in the late 1950s, George Sugarman and Ronald Bladen). Thus Held continued to paint and repaint his color-forms in flat coats until they possessed weight and felt right. What was more important, repeated adjustment enabled Held to make each of them specific or individuated—unique—that is, unrelated to any other. Furthermore, each color-forms was muscled into its own space by its adjoining color-forms as it muscled them into theirs, this contributing to the specificity of them all. The energy of a separable, specific form is more *frontal,* figuratively striking the eye head on, than *lateral,* as is the energy generated by forms related in shape and color which draw the eye across the picture surface. The opticality of color and the tactility of discrete, massive, opaque forms tend to conflict, but Held made them augment each other, to the extent that the *carrying power* of his

paintings surpassed that of any of his contemporaries, as Fairfield Porter observed. *Held projects like a great actor.*[4]

Held also came to prefer specific forms dissociated from each other because he wished to avoid the *rhythmic repetition* related to Cubist design, an organizing principle that struck him as used up. It was primarily in his large-scale pictures of this period that he achieved an unprecedented, disjunctive structure. More than any other quality in his painting, the specificity of Held's color-forms made it new. His need was to transform squares, triangles, and circles, which were by their nature generalized, indeed, the most generalized of shapes, into particular forms. In this, he was motivated by a new conception of content: the complex meanings that a nonobjective pictorial *language* could convey. Held's primary aim was not to fashion an easily identifiable style—although he achieved that—but to formulate a fresh content whose dimensions are philosophical as well as esthetic. That is, he aspired willfully to invest each of his color-forms with an individual character and presence as if each was a real being.

Held's transformation of geometric figures into anthropomorphic metaphors distinguished his abstraction from that of Louis, Noland, and Stella. Although each of the latter evolved an independent style, they shared a purist intention: to eliminate from painting all that was not of its medium, a reductive intention that was widely considered avant-garde or mainstream in the 1960s. During this decade, purist dogmas, particularly those advanced by Clement Greenberg on the one hand and on the other, critics disposed to Stella's work dominated art critical discourse. Stella's paintings, composed of centered, concentric stripes, are self-referential, deduced from the framing edges of the canvas. According to Greenberg, mainstream pictures were supposed to be thinly painted, pref-

erably stained, open color-fields, like Louis's and Noland's, since staining above all made color optical, and disembodied opticality was what pure painting ought to aspire to. Shapes broke up the field and were to be banished or, if used, were to be neutrally symmetrical and generalized, like Noland's circles, chevrons, and horizontal stripes, but certainly not like Held's obtrusive, off-centered, individuated geometry which resisted any spread into field. As Greenberg saw it, the future was with post-abstract expressionist opticality; the past with tactility. You were either for the one and against the other, no two ways about it.

Held's concrete color-forms, physical and energy packed rather than disembodied, impacted rather than open, were associated by purists with abstract expressionism. So were the signs of revisions, the ghosts of underpainting, in his somewhat uneven surfaces and edges. Curiously enough, purists accepted the painting process of Louis, Noland, and Stella, but because it was one-shot and no-hand; that is, it did not exhibit traces of correction. Held's pictures were largely ignored by the purists, yet the abstract expressionist camp was not much more sympathetic to his paintings, which it found too deficient in gesture and thus related to stained color-field abstraction and kindred purist tendencies. Held was relegated to an art critical limbo.

In the 1970s, the purist rhetoric of the 1960s lost its hold on art critical discourse. It became credible to entertain other conceptions of content and form, to see with a new eye, as it were. In this changed climate, Held's early abstractions will surely be appreciated as they were not when first shown.

—IRVING SANDLER

[1]*As early as Autumn 1958, Al Held wrote in "Panel,"* It Is 2 *(A Series of Statements Compiled by Irving Sandler), p. 78: "I would like to . . . [go] outward toward the spectator. The space between the canvas and the spectator is real—emotionally, physically and logically. It exists as an actual extension of the canvas surface. I would like to use it as such and thus bridge the gulf that separates the painting from the viewer."*

[2]*Held's process of painting is documented in Irving Sandler, "Al Held Paints A Picture,"* Art News, *May 1964. Sixteen of the stages of Genesis, 1963 the abstraction under discussion, are illustrated.*

[3]*Leger remarked on the debt he owed to the hand-painted ties on Broadway: a locomotive and four pigeons on a violet and black ground or a buxom nude on a saffron ground.*

[4]*Fairfield Porter, Talk at the New York Studio School, New York, April 28, 1967.*

1959 73"x37½

1959 $39\frac{1}{2}$″x39″

1959 57½″x39″

1959 39½"x37½"

1960 37½"x34"

1960 39½″x36¾″

1961 acrylic on paper 18″x24″

1961 acrylic on paper 18″x24″

1960 73¼″x37″

1960 73″x37½″

1960 42¼″x95½″

1960 acrylic on canvas 18″x26″

1960 acrylic on canvas 18″x14″

1961 77"x42"

1961 acrylic on paper 18″x24″

1961 acrylic on paper 18″x24″

1961 73″x42½″

1961 64″x42″

1961 74½″x42″

1960 acrylic on canvas 72″x48″

1961 73½″x42½″

Design: John Cheim
Consultation: Tara Collins of H.O. Gerngross & Co., Inc.
Lithography; Thorner Sidney Inc.